For Joseph and Gabriel N.D.
For Sophie E.S.

WALKER BOOKS
AND SUBSIDIARIES
LONDON · BOSTON · SYDNEY · AUCKLAND

First published 2020 by Walker Books Ltd, 87 Vauxhall Walk, London SE11 5HJ • This edition published 2021 • 10 9 8 7 6 5 4 3 2 1
Text © 2020 Nicola Davies • Illustrations © 2020 Emily Sutton • The right of Nicola Davies and Emily Sutton to
be identified as author and illustrator respectively of this work has been asserted by them in accordance with the
Copyright, Designs and Patents Act 1988 • This book has been typeset in Gill Sans MT • Printed in China

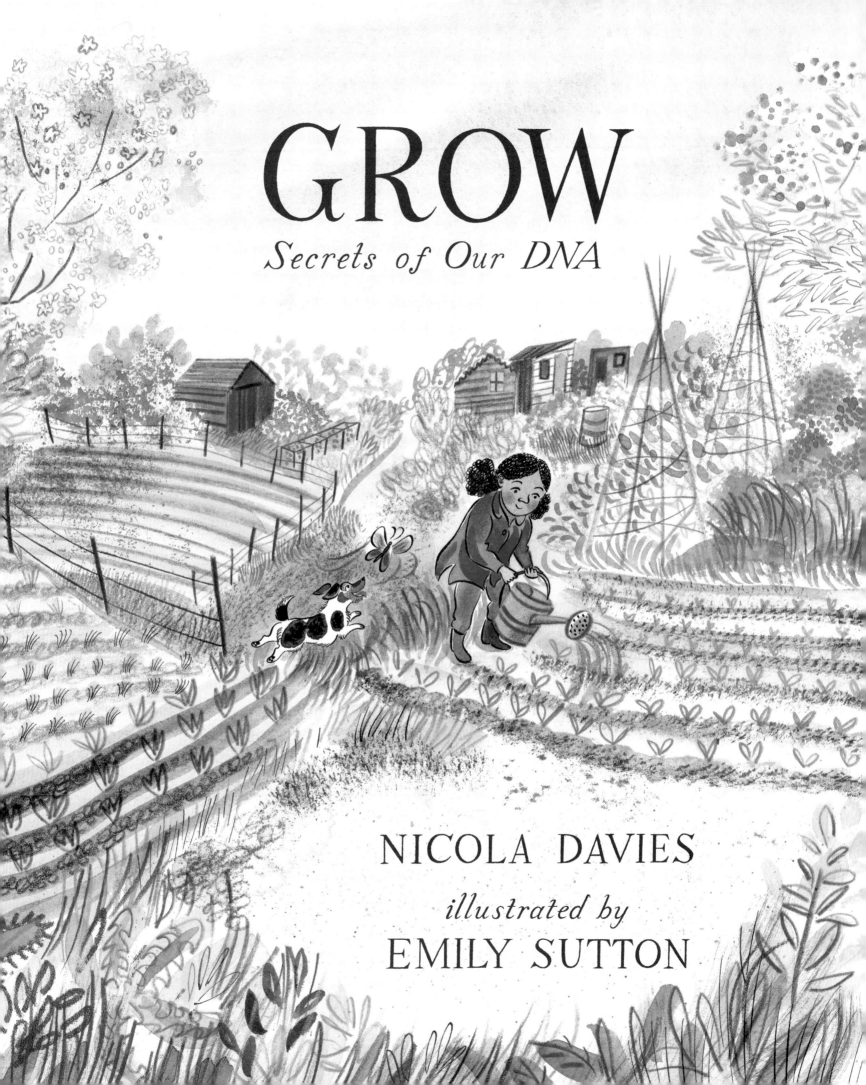

GROW
Secrets of Our DNA

NICOLA DAVIES

illustrated by

EMILY SUTTON

All living things **grow**.

Plants …

animals …

and humans.

The way they grow helps them to survive in different places.
Some grow fast, to make the most of good times …

Desert four o'clock plants make
the most of rare showers of rain by growing
from seed to flower in just ten days.

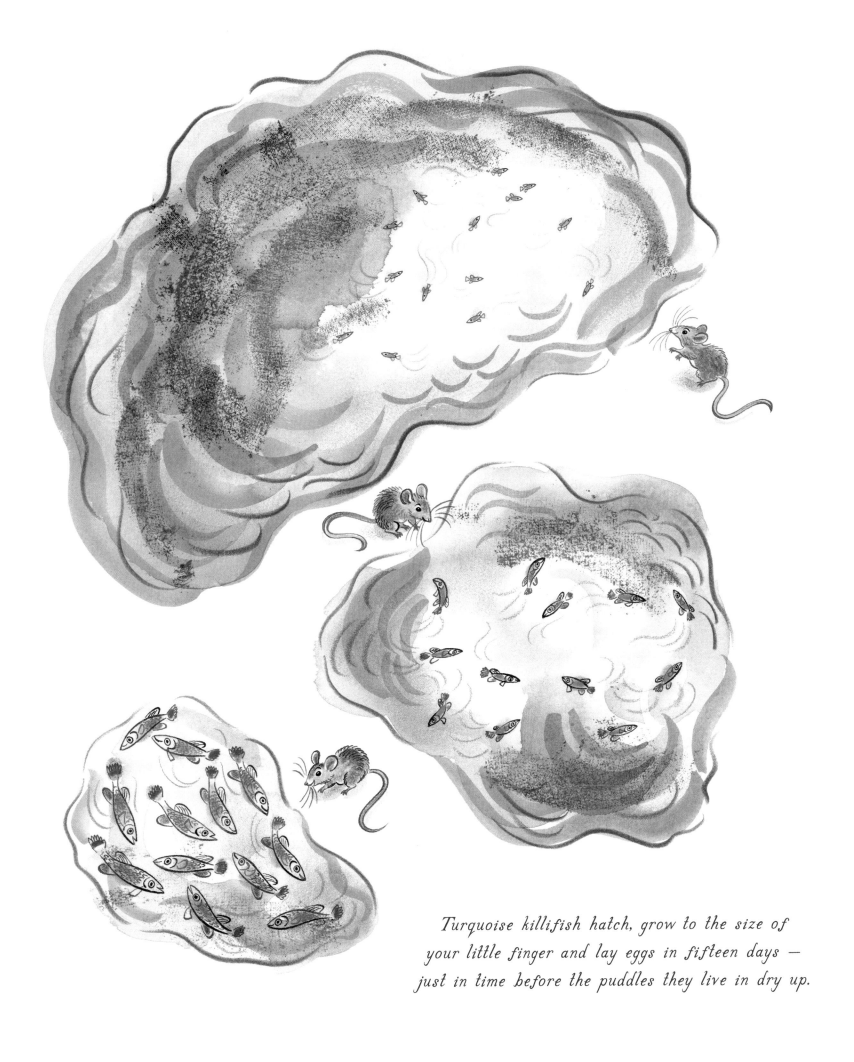

Turquoise killifish hatch, grow to the size of
your little finger and lay eggs in fifteen days —
just in time before the puddles they live in dry up.

and others grow slowly,
so they can keep going
when times are tough.

*Bristlecone pines endure harsh mountain conditions
by taking 40 years to grow to the size of a pencil.
They live for more than 4,000 years.*

In the deep Arctic Ocean, where it's always cold and dark, quahog clams can take 500 years to grow to be as big as your palm.

How **much** things grow is important too. Some never get very big, while others grow to be **enormous**.

Sunfish and leaf chameleons start life pretty small ...

*but chameleons must live under leaves,
so they never grow longer than a matchstick.*

Sunfish have the whole ocean to swim in — and they can grow to be huge!

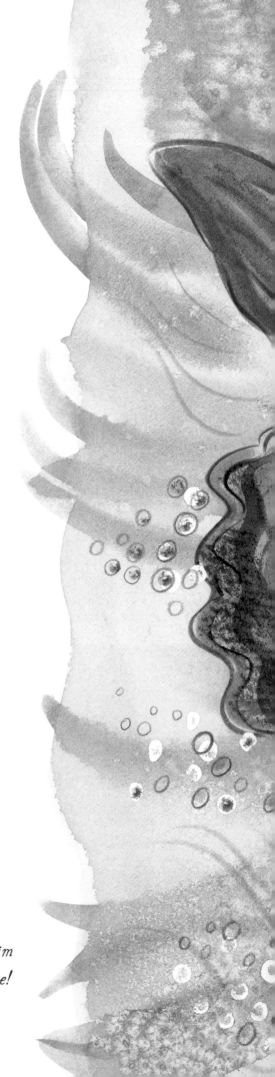

And growing isn't only about size.
It's about change.

Seeds don't grow into bigger seeds, but into
trees and flowers. Caterpillars turn into butterflies.

You grew from a tiny blob,
smaller than a dot, inside your
mum's tummy.

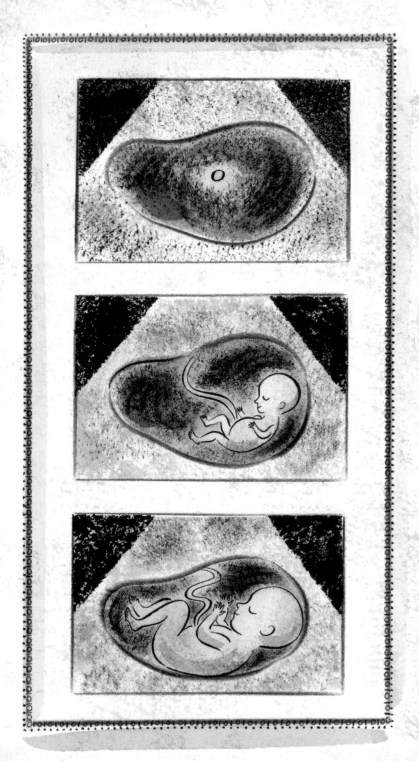

2 DAYS OLD

6 YEARS OLD

10 YEARS OLD

But your body didn't just get bigger. It changed shape, becoming more complicated and able to do more things.

You will go on growing and changing as you become an adult.
You won't have to think about it, or tell your body what to do,
because right from when you were dot-sized, your body has
been following a set of instructions.

These instructions aren't written in words, but in a code – made from something called DNA.

If you could see DNA it would look like a spiral ladder, with different kinds of steps.

DNA BASES

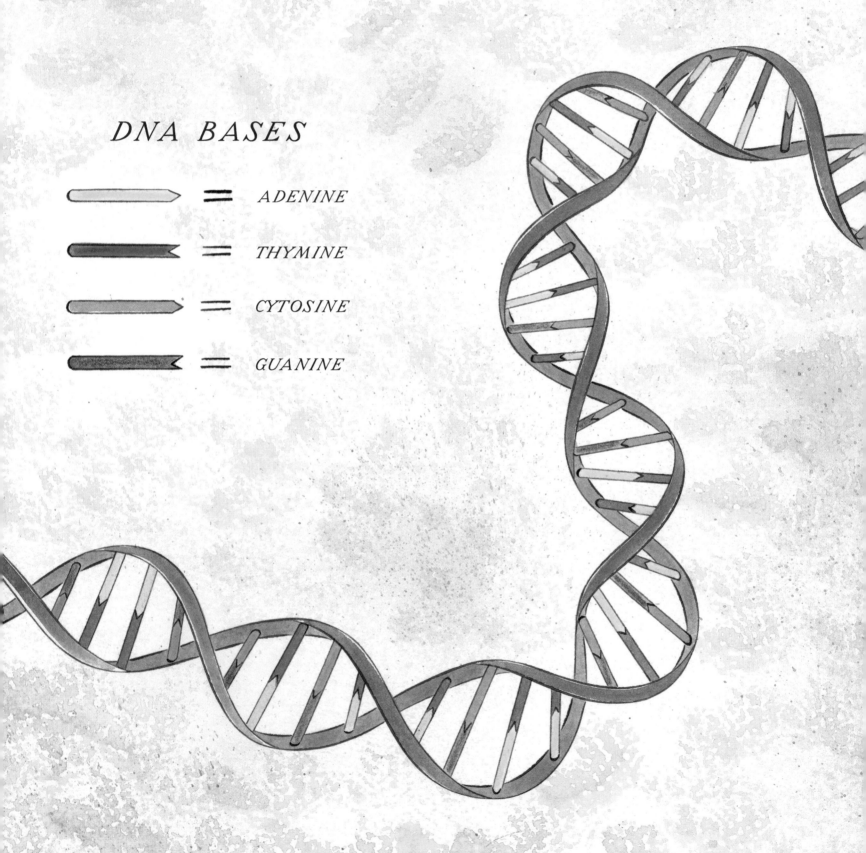

ADENINE

THYMINE

CYTOSINE

GUANINE

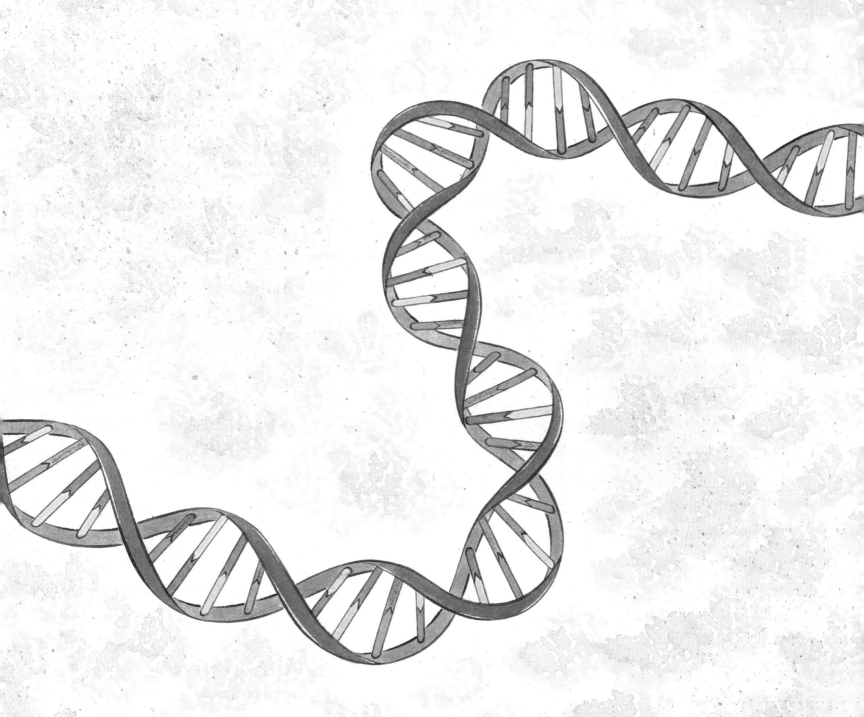

There are four kinds of steps, shown here in different colours.
The spiral ladder of DNA has thousands and thousands of
steps, so these four kinds can be ordered in many, many ways.

The pattern of the steps creates the coded instructions to build bodies. We call that pattern the "genetic code", and we call each instruction a "gene".

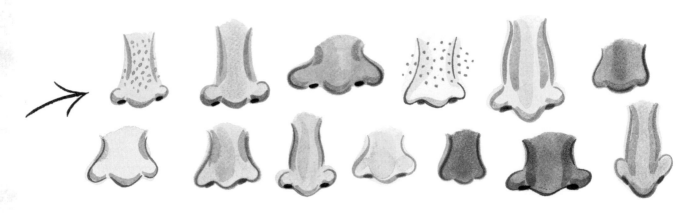

4 genes to shape a nose.

More than 100 genes to help to control hair colour and texture.

At least 16 genes give eyes their colour.

It takes more than 20,000 genes, working together in
the right order, to build a human body and keep it running.
That's about two metres of DNA.

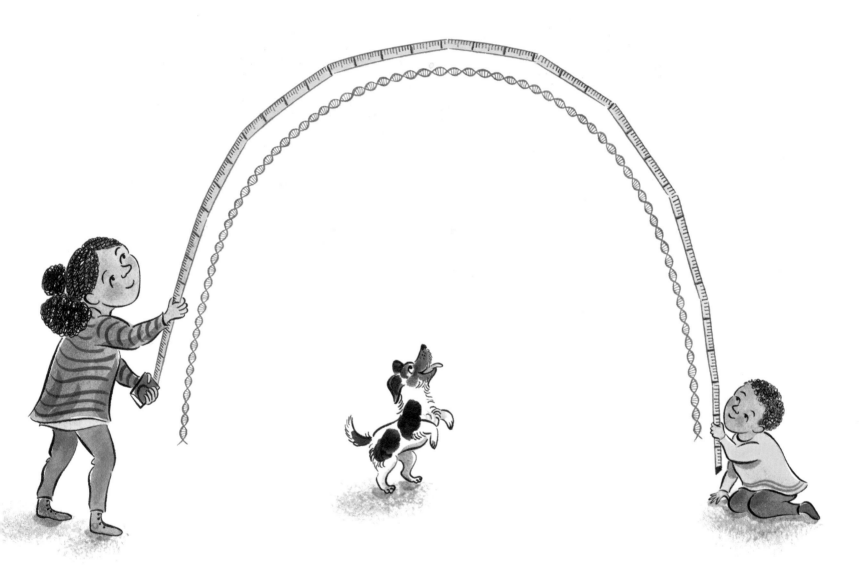

Luckily DNA is very skinny, and folds up so small that you'd
need a microscope to see it. That's how a copy of your genetic
code fitted inside you when you were just a dot – and how it
fits inside almost every one of the cells that make your body.

Half of your genetic code comes from your biological dad and half from your biological mum – that's why you may look a bit like both of them.

The exact mixture of instructions that you get from your parents isn't exactly like your brothers' or sisters' (unless you have an identical twin!). It's unique.

By studying how similar or different genetic codes are, scientists can tell who's related to who. Although your genetic code is unique, it's very similar to that of your family, and shows that you are closely related. It's also quite similar to the genetic code of every other person on Earth, because we are all human beings.

Animals and plants have a genetic code too.

Human genetic code is very like the genetic
code of chimpanzees, our closest animal relatives.
It's less like dog genetic code …

even less like that of a goldfish …

and much less like that of a rose!

But we share some parts of our genetic code with all living things. Those that are alive now, and all those that have ever lived on Earth.

Although we are so different, our DNA shows us that we are all part of life's big family.

Our DNA connects us with each other and to our ancestors,
back through time to the very start of life on Earth ...

because all life has always been
written in one language.

Afterword: How Did You Grow?

Your body is made of tiny units called "cells". You began life as a single cell. By the time you were born, you were made of 26 billion cells – and by the time you are an adult, you'll be made of almost 2,000 times as many as that.

You began growing when two cells – an egg cell from your mum and a sperm cell from your dad – joined together to make one cell. The DNA inside these cells joined up too, and the long DNA string bunched up into fat sausages called "chromosomes".

The chromosomes then split down the middle and the cell split into two …
    and two into four …
    and four into eight …
    and eight into sixteen.
This splitting is called "mitosis".

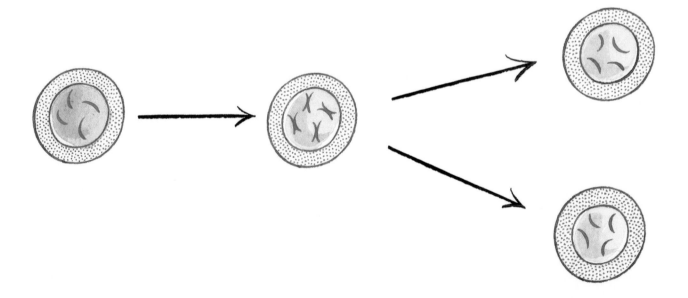

At first the new cells were all the same, but soon the instructions in your DNA started to make them into different kinds of cells. There are over 200 different kinds of cells in your body including:

• muscle cells that help you to move

• nerve cells that carry messages round your body

• brain cells that connect to each other, so you can think

• skin cells that protect your body

• blood cells that carry oxygen to every part of your body

That's how all the different parts of you began to grow!

Also by Nicola Davies and Emily Sutton:

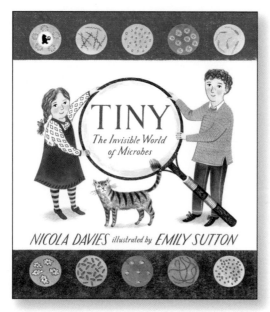

ISBN 978-1-4063-6070-7

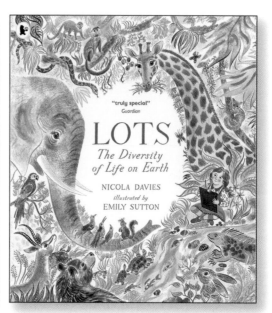

ISBN 978-1-4063-7889-4

Available from all good booksellers

www.walker.co.uk